COBALT

THE LEGACY OF THE BLACKBIRD MINE

Russell Steele

ISBN-10: 0972910808
EAN: 9780972910804

First printing 2009

Permissions and acknowledgements appear on p. 98.

Book and cover design by Caitlin Steele. Typeset in Minion Pro.

The Insightworks
PO Box 1569
Nevada City, CA 95959

Dedication

This book is dedicated to all the people who contributed stories, pictures, and the other material contained in this book, especially Bob and Alberta Wiederrick who invested many hours searching for photos and source material. Without everyone's help, friendship, and dedication I could not have completed this project.

I am especially thankful to my wife Ellen who was my companion, and editor, as we searched for the stories and pictures for this book. And, to my four wonderful daughters for their support; Jessica, Rachael, Heather and especially Caitlin for designing the book cover and the layout.

And, to all those who asked, "When will the book be done?"

Table of Contents

   Cobalt Memories. See page 96 for instructions on Internet access to Chapter Six and all future chapters.

Forward

Welcome to an interactive experiment in recording and sharing the history of the Blackbird Mine, and Cobalt, the town the mine created on the banks of Panther Creek. I have collected more material, photos and videos, than I can put in a single book of any practical size. Most readers will just want some information about the Blackbird Mine. Others may be interested in stories about Cobalt and the people who lived there.

This booklet is a chronological history of the Blackbird mine. Buy this book and you will also have exclusive access to a web site with stories about living at the Blackbird, building the town of Cobalt, life in Cobalt in its prime, and during it's decline and eventual demise under the auction gavel.

These are my stories, and the stories shared with me by the people who lived at Cobalt. I could not put them all in one book, as the price would exceed what most people will pay for this kind of information. However, the cost of publishing on the world wide web is quite low, thus allowing me to publish more stories, color photos, plus video and audio clips. On the Internet, I can link to supporting material. After reading the web pages, perhaps others will share their stories, which will add more depth to the story of the Blackbird Legacy. In the back of the book you will find a pass key to the Cobalt Memories web site.

INTRODUCTION

This history was compiled from multiple sources of varying reliability. Primary sources include the annual reports submitted by mining companies which worked in the Blackbird Canyon. The Idaho State Inspector of Mines reports from 1913 to 1962. The State Mine Inspectors Office was disbanded by the Idaho legislature in 1974, ending this official source of documentation.

Early reports include those written by Idaho State Mine Inspector Robert Bell in 1918, and Joseph B. Umpleby in 1913. The United States Geological Survey, Bulletin 528 Geology and Ore Deposits of Lemhi County was written by Umpleby, based on field work starting in 1910, and the work of other geologists and mining engineers. He devotes six pages to the Blackbird District.

Other resources include mining journals, magazines, newspapers and company newsletters. I hope the unpublished interviews and personal experiences add depth to the official reports which can be rather dry, lacking a sense of the human events that made the Blackbird such an interesting place to live and work. Where sources are in conflict, I have tried to resolve the dates and clarify events, however some ambiguity may still exist.

MINE HISTORY

THE BLACKBIRD DISTRICT

The Blackbird District covers rugged mountainous terrain, with flat top ridges, some a mile or more wide, mixed with sharp ridges, some reaching 8,200 feet. The ridge tops are separated by narrow V shaped rocky canyons, bordered by scattered bluffs and steep piles of sharp talus. Flat top ridges surround the Blackbird Canyon.

The Blackbird Canyon above the mouth of Meadow Creek is wider, with moderate soil-matted slopes, more open than the deeper canyon below the mine. Below Meadow Creek, the canyon narrows, with some wider flat spots, especially were the West fork of Blackbird Creek enters the main stream. Both Meadow Creek and Blackbird Creek are year round streams, part of the Panther Creek drainage which flows north to the Salmon River.

(Idaho Geological Survey, University of Idaho)

Location of Blackbird Mine and town of Cobalt

All Blackbird claims are above 6,000 feet. The surrounding mountains are covered in lodge pole pine, fir and spruce. Some of the lodge pole pine groves are so thick it is impossible to walk through the forested areas, the fallen trees piled like children's jackstraws. Lower down the talus slopes dominate with patches of native grass, sage brush and quivering aspen groves. Willows thrive along the creek banks, where mine tailings have not poisoned the roots.

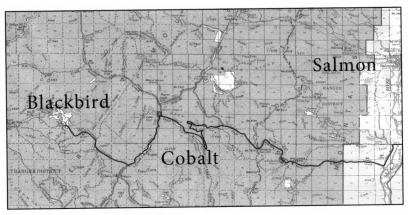

(US Forest Service map, showing route from Salmon the Cobalt and Blackbird mine.)

The winters are long, lasting from November through March, with winter temperatures rarely rising above 25 degrees, with short periods when the temperature drops to zero. At these temperatures, unprotected flesh sticks to exposed metal. Every breath produces a personal vapor cloud that freezes to beards and cloth. The average winter snow fall is about three to four feet, which is often gone by mid May, summers are short and are pleasant, however frost can occur any time. Summer average temperatures are 63 degrees.

Due to the high altitude, a daily temperature shift of 40 degrees can occur in both summer and winter. With all the Blackbird claims located from six to eight thousand feet, winter conditions existed a good six months of the year, and summer snow storms were not unknown.

The region was named by Samuel James in 1890 while seeking placer gold in the region. He named the creek Blackbird after some tame blackbirds that came to his campsite to pick up crumbs.

Brewers Blackbird (Photo from University of Utah Collection)

The Idaho Cobalt Belt is a thirty five mile long zone containing Pre-Cambrian rocks enriched in cobalt, copper and gold. The ICB runs from south east to north west through the Blackbird Creek Canyon. The sedimentary rocks were deposited about 1.5 million years ago in a basin covering most of northern Idaho and parts of Montana. The copper, cobalt and gold were extruded through the basin floor as hot liquid, similar to the "black smokers" observed on the sea floor today. Later arriving sediment covered the minerals and applied pressure, which combined with heat from below metamorphosed into the formations that exist today, after they were uplifted and erosion exposed the minerals to the miners seeking wealth in the Blackbird Canyon.

DISCOVERY

MINERAL DISCOVERIES ON BLACKBIRD CREEK—1892 TO 1893.

The Blackbird District mineralization was discovered by a Lemhi Indian named Little Tommy in 1892. Only one of a few verified native american mineral discoveries in Idaho, according to the Idaho Historical Society.

On a hunting trip Tommy became lost in a lodge-pole thicket. Seeking a clearing to gain his bearing he climbed to a ridge top and came across an outcrop of copper ore, green rocks exposed on the forest floor. These loose stones with exposed minerals are called float by geologists.

This discovery was witnessed in 1893 by Robert Bell, a noted mining expert who staked the first claim in the district. Bell later became the State Mine Inspector, an elected position.

In Bell's own words:

"The Blackbird District was discovered by a Lemhi Indian

Robert Bell, Idaho Mine Inspector (Photo provided by Idaho Historical Society) known as Little Tommy, who told a story of 'a mountain top strewn with 'money rock' which proved . . . true in its fullest details."

In October of 1893, with Little Tommy as a guide, Bell made a three day trip from Salmon Hot Springs to the Blackbird Creek Canyon to confirm the "money rock" discovery.

"The discovery was reached after a rather strenuous cross country trip through lots of timber and the third day out displayed a rich array of green stained copper carbonate float with splendid kidneys of very high grade red oxide of copper and subsequently proved to be on the divide between the head of Blackbird Creek and the Little Deer Creek.

I made a hurried location of the discovery ground and called it the Indian Claim. Today the Indian claim is the central point of a belt connecting lode claims, that covered the area of mountain ridges and canyons fifteen miles in length and from three to five miles wide."

The ore sample collected by Bell assayed at sixty eight percent copper and fifty four percent gold.

After Bell staked his claim, the next claim was staked by Samuel James in August of 1894. The district was soon flooded by prospectors who filed multiple copper and gold claims. In 1895, J.O. Swift invested $12,000 in the Uncle Sam Group, agreeing to build a five stamp-mill for half interest.

In 1896 Auto Stalmann took an option on the Uncle Sam on behalf of Glasgow & Western and spent $15,000 in development work. The option expired and the mine was sold to the Blackbird Copper Gold Mine in 1899 for $70,000.

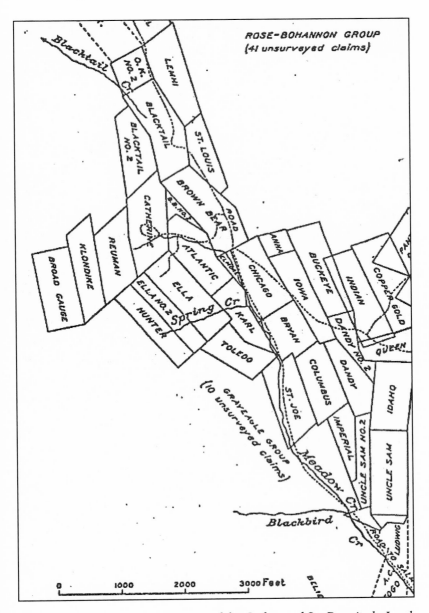

Section of a claims map of Lemhi County Idaho, Geology and Ore Deposits, by Joseph B. Umpleby, 1918.

Bell continued to work his claim. A tunnel was started and "at 50 feet copper pyrites commenced to show at a fact depth of seventy five feet. This tunnel showed a vein of blue sulfide over three feet wide worth 25 percent copper and $20.00 gold per ton," wrote William Bell.

Log cabins at the mouth of Blackbird Creek (Photo provided by Lemhi County Historical Society)

The Brown Bear was located in June 1895 by Ford and Brown working on a grub stake by Dr. Wright of Salmon. Wright took samples East and found a group of investors, C. North of Buffalo NY and M. Gilbert of Chicago, IL, who took a two year option. After traveling to Salmon to confirm the Brown Bear claims, these investors took options on other claims in the Blackbird Canyon. They sold the Brown Bear Group and 40 other claim groups for $250,000 to John E. Dubois, Dubois, Pennsylvania, and associates from Buffalo, NY and Boston, MA.

William Bell described the Blackbird District in the Salt Lake Tribune, December 1900, reprinted in the Salmon Recorder January 1901.

"Most of the vein croppings were filled with a soft, spongy brown oxidized quartz that panned well in free gold. This was particularly true of the Uncle Sam vein, also the Ella, Brown Bear, Chicago, Columbia and St. Joe, and most of the prospectors that they had a free milling gold camp."

BLACKBIRD CAMP AND EARLY DAYS

BLACKBIRD COPPER GOLD MINING COMPANY—1899 TO 1901

The Dubois purchases on upper Blackbird and Meadow Creeks included the Brown Bear #1 and #2, Blacktail #1 and #2, St. Joe and Uncle Sam #1 and #2 and the Chicago. The investors established the Blackbird Copper and Gold Mining Co, and built a camp on Blackbird Creek.

Log cabins at the mouth of Blackbird Creek (Photo provided by Lemhi County Historical Society)

The Blackbird Camp included a Post Office, company store and seventy five miners, prospectors and some families living along the banks of the creek in tents and hand hewn log cabins. The 1900 Census listed 90 people living at the Blackbird. The Post Office closed in 1906, as the miners left to seek their fortune elsewhere.

The last Blackbird Postmaster was Ed Hines, who was also the Dubois property manager, handling the payroll and operating the company commissary. By 1910, the census listed only 20 people living in the community. Ed stayed on as the Dubois property caretaker until the mine closed, then moved to a ranch along the Salmon River, where he lived out the rest of his life. Most active mining ceased in 1901, due to the remote location and high cost of operation.

Ed Hines with salmon he caught by hand at the mouth of Blackbird Creek.
(Photo provided by Lemhi County Historical Society)

Blackbird Creek Camp, specific date unknown. (Photo provided by Lemhi County Historical Society)

Supplies had to be brought from Salmon by wagon or pack mule, over mountain passes that were only open in the summer. Snow drifts 20 feet deep on the summits were not uncommon. A pack trip often took three days to reach the mine, and three days to return to Salmon with the ore concentrate. Pack trains ranged in size from 4 to 125 mules depending on the cargo to be carried. The first leg was from Salmon up the steep ridge tops directly west, into the timber and over the summit down to Leesburg.

The second leg was from Leesburg to the Leecock Ranch Station where Napias Creek spills into Panther Creek. The trail was very steep and in many places carved into the cliff face. On one side a frothy stream hundreds of feet below and a shear rock cliff on the other. One misstep and there was no way to recover. The third leg was up Panther Creek, then called Big Creek, to the mouth of Blackbird Creek and the mines up the creek. Prospecting in the area continued as individual miners proved out their claims. In September of 1917, Charles Shultz, Wiley Rose, and Walter Rose were the only hardy prospectors still struggling to make a living in the Blackbird Canyon, according to a report by the Mine Inspector. They were prospecting for gold and copper.

HAYNES-STELLITE OPERATION —1901 TO 1940

In 1901, James Bellile, a local prospector and French citizen, staked fourteen cobalt claims on the West Fork of Blackbird Creek. These claims were about four miles from the mouth of Blackbird Creek, and about two miles below the present Blackbird mine. Over time, seven additional claims were staked northward across the main stream of Blackbird Creek, bringing the total to twenty one.

In 1915, James Caples, a local engineer and surveyor, with financing from Haynes-Stellitte of Kokomo, Indiana, procured ten of these claims for $10,000 cash on the north side of Blackbird Creek. Elwood Haynes was a prolific inventor, credited with the first gasoline powered car, the household thermostat, and the development of stainless steel. However, his most important invention was stellitte, a malleable alloy of cobalt and chromium. A combination which opened the door to the development of a series of space age alloys of the highest melting temperatures, which could operate in high stress applications such as high speed cutting tools, valve seats and jet engine blades, all while resisting corrosion. The Haynes-Stellitte mine was the early source of cobalt for this signature product. It was also the first time cobalt became the mineral of interest in the Blackbird Canyon.

By 1917, under the direction of James Caples a ten stamp mill was erected at the Haynes Camp, also referred to as the Blackbird Camp in some pictures and writing. The mill processed 100,000 pounds of 17.7 percent concentrate in 1918-1919. In the fall of 1919 a 200 KW hydroelectric plant on Panther Creek, two miles down stream from the mouth of Napias Creek, went online to supplement steam powered generators and a diesel compressor at the Haynes Camp.

This new capability came online shortly before Union Carbide bought Haynes-Stellite and closed down the mine. Concentrate processing problems and the high cost of operating the mine were cited as the reasons for the closure. In 1917, cobalt metal was selling for $1.50 to $2.00 and cobalt oxide $1.00 to $1.50 per pound.

Blackbird camp buildings and mill (Photo provided by Lemhi County Historical Society)

World War I (1914–1818) increased the demand for cobalt, making mining necessary and feasible. Cobalt was needed to harden aircraft engine valve seats, manufacture high-speed metal cutting tools and powerful magnets for electric motors. Once the war was over the need for cobalt diminished rapidly, resulting in falling cobalt prices.

The remote location, forty miles from the rail head in Salmon, over snow covered mountain passes in the winter, increased operating costs. In 1920 Haynes-Stellite, by then a division of Union Carbide, suspended operations. According to the Mine Inspector's records, the company continued to file reports and pay taxes until Union Carbide discovered the patented claims were invalid in the mid 1920s, and stopped payment.

From 1920 to 1940, very little mining was done along Blackbird Creek and its tributaries, except for annual assessments on unpatented claims and some prospecting. In 1939 the Haynes-Stellitte properties were relocated by J.G. Sims of Salmon and F. W. Stevenson of Forney, Idaho. The Haynes-Stellitte patents had been declared invalid in the mid 1920s by a Judge.

UNCLE SAM MINING AND MILLING COMPANY —1937 TO 1940

In 1937, most of the Duboise claims were sold by Lemhi County to J.G. and J.H. Sims of Salmon, for back taxes. In 1938 the Uncle Sam Mining and Milling Company was formed by F. W. Stevenson who leased 42 claims from the Sims', opening up two old tunnels on the Uncle Sam claim. The company was prospecting for cobalt, copper and gold, according to the mine inspectors reports. A seventy five ton per day flotation mill was built near the Uncle Sam portal in 1940. The primary power was supplied by gasoline

Blackbird Mine mill in 1940 (Photo provided by Lemhi County Historical Society, from the Herb St Clair collection)

and diesel engines. Sixteen men were employed at the mine. In 1941 the only production was 21 tons of copper concentrate shipped to the smelter from the Uncle Sam Mine.

Concentrate bin at the mouth of Blackbird Creek (Photo provided by Lemhi County Historical Society, from the Herb St Clair collection)

By May of 1942 only four men were working at the mine. Uncle Sam Mining and Milling Company recovered 163, 485 pounds of copper, 332 ounces of silver and 461 ounces of gold. Cobalt in the copper concentrates was undesirable and resulted in penalties at the smelter. By fall of 1942 all operations had lapsed, again due to the cost of operation in a remote location, even though a road had been built and the supplies brought in by truck.

CRITICAL MINERALS AND THE WAR DAYS

HOWE SOUND COMPANY AND CALERA MINING COMPANY—1943 TO 1959

The price of Cobalt in 1942 was $1.50 per pound. The Bureau of Mines started a diamond drilling and trenching program, part of a war time strategic minerals program, to determine the scope of the cobalt deposits in the Blackbird District. By 1945, they had bulldozed numerous trenches to expose the underlying formation and had drilled 11,000 feet of diamond drill holes. Copper was $12.00 per pound and was needed to support the emerging cold war.

Howe Sound optioned the Sims properties in the summer of 1943, and started their own diamond drilling program near the Brown Bear property under the supervision of Engineer Cecil Whitley. From 1943 to 1945, the United States Geological Survey did extensive surface and underground mapping of the cobalt deposit along the east side of Meadow Creek. By the summer of 1944, Howe Sound was convinced that the Cobalt deposit was large enough to invest in underground exploration. However, due to war time man power shortages the work was delayed until the summer of 1945.

In 1945, the underground exploration work was done by the Calera Mining Company, a division of Howe Sound. Calera had completed 11,537 feet of tunnels by the spring of 1947. The newest structures on site were some war surplus Quonset huts converted into quarters for families living at the mine. Electrical power was provided by a diesel generator, located near the 6,800 level audit.

With the ore reserves confirmed, Howe Sound made plans to bring electrical power to the site and start a major construction program at the mine. A meadow along Panther Creek, six mines from the mine, was purchased from the Jones Family for a town site. Also to be serviced by the 90 mile 69KW power line running from Bannack Montana to Salmon, Idaho, and then over the mountain to the Blackbird Mine and the town site. The estimate cost

Blackbird Camp 1947, from color 16 mm film by Harry W. Marsh.
(Film proided by Idaho Historical Society)

was $680,000. The final bill would be about a million dollars according to T.E. Roach, President of the Idaho Power Company, who built the power line. The leg from Salmon to the mine and town site cost $477,500 according to reports in the Salmon Recorder-Herald.

Two years later, in the spring of 1949, Calera reported having completed 18,428 feet of tunnel, crosscuts and drifts and major infrastructure improvements were under construction. By the end of summer in 1950, Calera had built a dry and change building, machine shop, warehouse and office building near the confluence of Blackbird and Meadow Creeks. Construction of a 600 ton per day mill was started, with the concrete foundation completed and ready for the erection of a steel building. Idaho Power completed the 69KW power transmission line to the mine site. Calera reported completing dormitories, dining hall, apartments, heating plant and residences by the spring of 1950 at the town site, anticipating the water systems, fire lines, and sewage disposal systems would be complete by the fall of that year, according to mine inspector reports.

By 1951, the Chicago tunnel complex was in full operation and the price of cobalt was $2.18, copper $2.50. Calera built a tailings impoundment dam on the West Fork of Blackbird creek and laid a concrete pipe to bring the tailings from the mill to the impoundment dam. Prior mining operation dumped the tailings in Blackbird Creek, causing significant environmental damage to the stream. In addition, the two mile long pipe, laid next to the stream, often burst when rocks rolled down the mountain striking the pipe, flooding the creek with more tailings. Water from the West Fork was pumped in relays up to the mill in wooden pipes.

Once the barracks buildings at the town site were completed, and busses

New metal buildings about 1950, on Meadow Creek (Photo provide by Idaho Geological Survey, University of Idaho)

to transport miners from the town site to the mine arrived, the bunk and cook house at the mine was closed. The miners now had access to comfortable barracks buildings at the town site with meals served at in a modern dining hall. A new ambulance was purchased in the spring by the Calera and a new two bed clinic opened for use by miners and their families.

By June of 1951, the 600 ton per day mill was completed and started and the first ore processed. The first shipment of copper concentrate was transported by truck to the railhead in Mackay, Idaho. The copper concentrate was placed in large metal buckets, with five buckets on a flatbed trailer. Cobalt concentrate was being stockpiled on site, waiting for the smelter to be completed at Garfield, Utah. In October, at the Government's request production was expanded to 1000 tons per day, which required fifty additional miners be hired by the company to meet this new demand.

In 1951, a total of 761 tons of copper concentrate, containing 101 ounces of gold and 106 ounces of silver were shipped to the smelter. Some cobalt was processed, but none was shipped.

The mill, crusher, and bin foundations took 20,000 sacks of cement to complete. The prefabricated mill, 283 tons of steel was used to protect the equipment and workers from the cold and snow that comes each winter to the Blackbird Canyon. In mid July, 1951, an 800 acre fire came with in 200 yards of this new mill.

By 1952, mill operations had been fine tuned and the mill was processing both copper and cobalt, but technical problems at the new refinery in

Garfield, Utah delayed cobalt shipments. Key components were subject to excessive corrosion and abrasion, resulting in mechanical failures. The refinery was built by Chemical Construction Corporation, a division of American Cyanamid, with work starting in 1948. With intermittent operation, the Garfield plan produced 591,500 pounds of cobalt. A total of 21,254 pounds of nickel was recovered from the cobalt concentrates.

The miners voted to be represented by the Mine, Mill and Smelter Workers and began negotiations resulting in a pay hike of 19.5 cents per hour. The town of Cobalt was identified as a Critical Defense Housing Area, which made the town site eligible for government housing.

Mining and milling operations were curtailed in 1953 due to continuing problems in bringing the Garfield, Utah smelter on line. Approximately 100 of the 250 workers were laid off.

Blackbird Mine Office in 1953. (Photo provided by Lyle Greig)

Dial telephones were installed at the town site including the clinic and mine offices; plus department head, maintenance and public official's homes, including the home of a Lemhi Deputy Sheriff. The phone was a carrier system, that operated over the power lines. There was a lot of background noise on the line, its usefulness was often determined by the weather. Local thunder storms made the line too noisy to use.

In 1953, seventy five housing units were completed by the Defense Housing Authority at the Cobalt town site.

In January, 1954, the miners laid off a year earlier were recalled. The labor force was projected to grow from 130 to 270 in three months, reaching 250 by April. A two year contract for additional cobalt-copper exploration was signed with the government. The Government advancing 75 percent, $394,843 of the $407,380 total, with repayment coming from royalties from the yet to be discovered ore.

Cobalt's Government housing units. (Photo provided by Lyle Greig)

By summer, Cobalt's population had reached 830, with citizens living in 168 homes, six apartments, three dormitories, and 75 government housing units. The Calara Chief Accountant, Hadden, predicted the population could grow to 1,200, possibly 1,800 in the future. As the population grew, the condition of the William Creek road became a larger issue for Cobalt residents relying on Salmon for their professional, medical, dental, and legal services. Cobalt miners and managers were spending an estimated $1.6 million a year for services and supplies in Salmon.

The Blackbird produced 631,397 pounds of cobalt and 25,726 pounds of nickel in 1954. Chemical Construction Corporation took over operation of the Garfield plant under a two year contract.

In May, 1955, the International Mine, Mill and Smelter workers went on strike for three weeks over a disputed firing, approximately 250 employees are working at the mine.

Technical problems at Garfield refinery were solved and production increased in 1956. With the technical difficulties solved, Calara took over operation of the Garfield plant in December of 1955. Even with operating problems the refinery produced 2.4 million pounds of cobalt and 98,495 pounds of nickel in 1956.

An electrolytic pilot plant proved successful, producing a higher quality of cobalt. A decision was made to built a full scale plant, estimates at about $750,000 at Garfield.

THE OPEN PIT

By April of 1957 an open pit was started. Isbell Construction Company was hired to operate the open pit. The pit sits on the saddle of Meadow Creek and Big Creek drainage. It produced 1,000 tons of ore per day, with 12,000 tons going to the spoils pile. Equipment used in the pit included two shovels, one of two and half yards and one of three yard capacity; eight Euclid, hauling twenty eight tons per load, three cats for clearing land, smoothing the dump and clean up around the shovel , one road patrol for road maintenance and two rotary drills. Blasting was done with ammonium nitrate, a commercial fertilizer mixed with diesel and primed with two pound charges of explosive and primer cord, all set off by an electric blasting cap.

The ore body was the same as the one being mined by underground methods. The open pit was soon producing more ore than the mill could process. When the open pit was complete, engineers forecast a two year stock pile would be stored near the mill. Copper concentrates was sent to a Tacoma, Washington smelter. The cobalt concentrates to Garfield, Utah. The ore was loaded in metal buckets, loaded on semi-flatbeds and hauled to the Mackay railhead. In 1957, 431 men are employed at the mine, producing 2.6 million pounds of cobalt.

In the Spring of 1958, the work force was 415 miners, including mill workers and open pit operators. The open pit and underground operations produced 3.1 million pounds of cobalt, with underground miners only working the first third of the year. In the fall of 1958, seventy underground miners were laid off and underground operations ceased; however, the open pit operations continued to produce copper and cobalt ore. Enough gold was smelted from

Start of the Open Pit in 1957 (Photo provided by Ted Maestretti, Isbell Project Supervisor)

the copper ore to pay open pit mining expenses, about 9,506 ounces. Nearly 3.1 million pounds of cobalt and 11 million pounds of copper were produced in 1958. By February of 1959, the open pit was mining only copper, with a combined staff of 135 workers at the mill and open pit. Lower grade copper ore was being stockpiled near the mill.

In May of 1959, the Government contract for $2.30 a pound for cobalt ended. The Korean war time need for cobalt and copper had passed, now the open market prevailed. The cobalt market price was $ 1.77, not enough to sustain the cost of operations at the Blackbird. Once again operating costs caused the closure of the mine.

Approximately 1.2 million pounds of cobalt were produced from stockpiled concentrates at the Garfield plant, completing the government contract. Garfield plant, which employed about 200 people, was closed in August, 1959.

By June, the staff was reduced to forty at the mine. The stockpiled low grade ore was processed for copper. The price of copper, $30.99 per pound. By the end of the year a staff of forty two operated the mill and eleven Isbell employees worked in the open pit. Lumber harvesting on mine property employed another eleven lumberjacks. On July 6, 1959, operation of the Blackbird was assumed by Misco P.C. Inc, New York, a holding company, and the mine ceased operations except for some care taking by eight employees. Assets included 41 patented claims, 396 unpatented claims, including 13 patented mill sites and 2 placer claims, according to Idaho's 60th Annual Mining Report.

Blackbird Mine mill in 1959 (Photo provided by Idaho Geological Survey, University of Idaho)

THE STRUGGLE TO KEEP THE MINE OPEN

BLACKBIRD MINE, MACHINERY CENTER INC.—1960 TO 1967

In the Spring of 1960, E. B. Douglas, the Calara Mining Company Manager since 1945, departed for Henderson, Nevada to manage Manganese Inc, a division of the Howe Sound Mining Company. It was the end of an era for the Blackbird.

All summer long, the Rowley Construction company was busy moving houses belonging to people in Cobalt to the Pahsimerol Valley, Challis and Salmon. In August, the school opened to serve the children of six families staying in Cobalt, hoping the mine would re-open.

In the fall of 1960, the town of Cobalt was purchased by Machinery Center, Inc., owned by Roger Pierce. The mine was leased from Howe Sound Company. No cobalt was produced in Idaho in 1960, as the Blackbird Mill and Mine remained idle. Misco P.C was liquidated at the end of 1960 and its assets transferred to the parent Howe Sound Company.

A dispute arose between the Lemhi Tax Collector and Misco P.C. over taxes owed to the County on profits for 1959. Misco P.C. claimed no profits, Lemhi County Tax collector requested $133, 282.44 based on projected profits of $1,894,562.13. Misco P.C. claimed a loss of over $4.7 million.

In 1961, Machinery Center bought more holdings including claims held by Howard Sims of Salmon, Calera, Northfield, South and Wider properties. Mine and mill were still idle, some mine machinery was sold to outside interests. Houses were bought and moved from the town-site. Misco P.C. paid portion of taxes owed to this County, $132,751.44. Liquidation of mine equipment continued, under the supervision of Jack Miller, who arrived in July. In the summer of 1961, the *New York Times* published a story on the rise and decline of Cobalt, in a story titled, "Infant Idaho Ghost Town."

In 1962, the Forest Service established a hell-attack base at Cobalt, "one of the best in the nation", according to a Forest Service inspector. The Machine Centers continued to buy more holdings in the Blackbird Canyon and surrounding drainages.

In 1963, Earl Waite and William Barnes were leasing the Blackbird No. 1 and Machinery Center, the Blackbird No. 2. The first shipment of copper concentrates was sent to the Mackay railhead, destined for the smelters at Tacoma, Washington and Anaconda, Montana. The Post Office Department assigned Zip Code 83229 to the Cobalt Post Office.

In 1964, the Cobalt School reopened with 22 students in seven grades. A December snow slide temporarily trapped miners at the 7,100 ft level, forcing them to seek an escape route through the 7,400 ft level, where they were challenged by bad ground and broken timbers. Once they escaped the mine, their return to Cobalt was blocked by snow slides between the mine and mouth of Blackbird Creek and again between the Panther Creek Inn and the town site. It was a long day for the trapped miners.

In 1965, the Machinery Center operated the mine (mostly the open pit) but did not recover cobalt, only copper and the gold in the copper concentrates. This operation caused a lot of damage including dumping tailings along the Blackbird Creek bed whenever the pipe to the tailings storage dam on the West Fork Blackbird Creek burst. Many of these accidents occurred at night, going undetected until the morning shift arrived for work. The 25 employees operating the mine and mill lived in Cobalt. The mill produced 1,438 tons of copper, 1,500 ounces of gold, and 3,224 ounces of silver. The Cobalt School opened with 42 students and two teachers, Mrs Smith and Mrs Miller.

In 1966, the tailings escaped from the holding dam on the West Fork of Blackbird Creek, during high water. This and other accidental spills became a growing concern of the Forest Service and Idaho Fish and Game. During high water the pipe under the 10 million tons of mine tailings could not handle the run off, resulting in the flood cutting into the waste pile and flowing over the spillway. Settling ponds below the spillway on the main branch of Blackbird Creek were over come by flood waters and tailings were carried into Panther Creek.

In October, the Salmon National Forest Advisory Council inspected the damage to Blackbird Creek and the flow of mine tailings silt into Panther Creek. They expressed concern that salmon could not be reintroduced to Panther Creek, until the mine waste was controlled in Blackbird Creek.

BLACKBIRD MINE

(HANNA MINING COMPANY- IDAHO MINING COMPANY, COASTAL MINING COMPANY) 1967 TO 1976

In June of 1967, Idaho Mining Company (Hanna) purchased fifty one percent of the Blackbird property on a two year development deal with the Machinery Center, and took over operation of the mine, launching a new exploratory program. Approximately eighty men were working at the mine and mill. At the peak of Idaho Mining Company's operations 105 were employed. They produced 2,916,200 pounds of copper, 1,880 ounces of gold and 33,387 ounces of silver. The Cobalt School opened with 45 pupils and three teachers, with grades one through eight.

The Deep Creek road from Williams Creek to Panther Creek officially opened, offering a longer, but safer trip from Cobalt to Salmon. The south facing slope would enhance winter driving conditions.

Roger Pierce dies, and Mrs. Pierce sells the remaining forty nine percent to the Idaho Mining company. The Machinery Center ceases to exist.

Idaho Fish and Game, and Idaho Department of Health expressed growing concern over silt flowing down Blackbird Creek into Panther Creek. A Fish and Game representative noted that the effluent coming into Panther Creek was cementing the stream bottom and turning it in to a physical and biological desert where no plants or bugs could live.

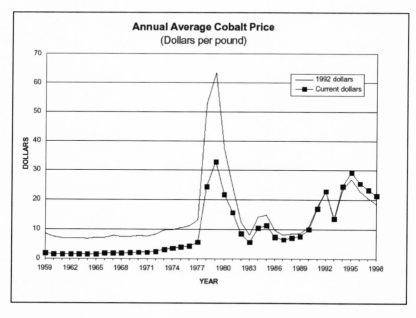

Cobalt price chart was provided by the Cobalt Development Institute. 167 High Street, Guildford, Surrey England

State officials attempted to set up minimum water quality standards for the Blackbird operation.

In 1968, a nationwide copper strike curtailed Blackbird production, however a diamond drilling program continued. The price of copper was $41.17 per pound.

Exploration in the summer of 1969 included more than a mile of tunnel, 400 feet of inclined shaft and several thousand feet of diamond drill holes. In the fall of 1969, the mine was closed and a caretaker hired to care for the property during the winter months.

In 1970, Idaho Mining Co, a subsidiary of Hanna Mining Company, conducted a feasibility study for reopening the Blackbird. The diamond drilling exploration ended in October, with the onset of winter.

In the summer of 1972, Hanna geologists again restarted the feasibility analysis, with a new diamond drilling program. The program was terminated with the onset of winter. There were no mining operations at the Blackbird in 1973.

In 1974, Idaho Mining Company continued exploration for cobalt and copper. The State of Idaho and Federal Agencies were taking a serious look at water pollution in Blackbird Creek, coming from the flooded mine and open pit. The Coastal Mining Company (a subsidiary of Hannah Mining Company) continued exploring for cobalt-nickel and cobalt-copper areas around the Blackbird through out 1975.

In 1976, the US government stopped selling cobalt from the strategic mineral stockpile, and cobalt production in Zaire was curtailed due to political unrest in the country. The price of cobalt rose to about $6.00 a pound. Exploration continued at the Blackbird by Coastal Mining.

The Cobalt Post Office in 1977. (Photo provided by Idaho Geological Survey, University of Idaho)

NORANDA DAYS AT THE BLACKBIRD

BLACKBIRD MINE (NORANDA MINING COMPANY) 1977 TO 1987

In 1977, Noranda Mines, Ltd. Toronto, Canada, saught options on the Blackbird, from Hanna. Zaire continues to constrain production and the price of cobalt started to rise in the global market, creating market instability in what had been quite stable in the 1960s and early 1970s, with prices on the rise. In 1978 the Shaba Province in Zaire was invaded by Zambia and the price of cobalt shot to $32.00 a pound on the global markets. The mining operations were shut down when the fighting resulted in damage that flooded the mines. African suppliers lose control of their market pricing power. Noranda, sensing an opportunity, leased the Blackbird Mine from the Hanna Mining Company.

In February, 1979, exploration and reconstruction continued with 15 men working at the Blackbird. By June, the work force had expanded to 70. The company was exploring locations for a new tailings pond. In Cobalt, two bunkhouses and dining hall were refurbished, providing rooms for 112 employees, however plans called for most employees to live in Salmon and commute to work by bus, if the Williams Creek road was improved.

By the fall of 1979, Noranda Exploration had spent $3.5 million and had refurbished 75% of the company buildings at the town site, and started to address environmental problems. The decision to put the mine into production was delayed, waiting for water discharge and diversion permits. In November, Noranda formed a US Company, Noranda Mining, Inc, to put the Blackbird mine into full production. The Forest Service decided that an environmental impact report would be required, because the tailings disposal pond needed to be moved.

In February, 1980, there were 125 persons working at the Blackbird, all but 20 commuting from Salmon. By October employment had risen to 170, with a 10 percent turn over. The four hours a day commute was hard on many miners and their families, and contributed to the turn overs. Monthly payroll was over $200,000 per month.

Noranda was investing a million dollars a month to rebuild the concentrator, continue underground and surface exploration and refurbish company buildings, including the town site. Cobalt reserves were estimated between 4.4 and 8.8 million pounds of cobalt, enough for twelve years of operation. A microwave telephone system was built from Salmon to the mine to improve mine safety communication.

A million dollar water treatment plant capable of processing 130,000 gallons, 400 gallons per minute, was built to clean up the acid water flowing from

Noranda water processing plant under construction. (Photo provided by Idaho Geological Survey, University of Idaho)

the mine at the 6,850-foot level. All mine drainage was diverted to the processing plant.

The Comprehensive Environmental Response, Compensation, and Liability Act (CERCLA) and the Super-Fund were passed by Congress and Signed by the President. Noranda funded the detailed environmental impact reports required by law, under Forest Service supervision in September, 1980. Public comments were solicited for mine operations in wilderness areas,

Blackbird Mine Mill from the air in 1980. (Photo from Irene Allen's private collection.)

especially those with potential heavy metal contamination of streams and rivers. The University of Idaho sent a team of students to test back-county streams for cobalt, copper and arsenic contamination. The study was funded by the National Science Foundation.

Cobalt went to $25 per pound at the beginning of 1980, but was under $20 per pound by years end. Copper was about $1 per pound.

At the beginning of 1981, 165 people were working at Blackbird for Noranda. Total investment to date was $30 million, including $1.3 million for the water treatment plant and $1.5 million to refurbish the mill. The Forest Service granted permission for operation of the mill at 30 tons per day for testing. Noranda took an option on 212 acres and started planning for a refinery in Bingham County, near Moreland, Idaho. This $60 million dollar investment was put on hold when the price of Cobalt remained under $20 a pound, making investment funding scarce. Cobalt was selling at $15 a pound on world markets. When efforts to gain a government subsidy failed, to hike the price to $22 pound, Noranda started laying off miners. By years end, only 65 employees were working at the Blackbird.

By the fall of 1982, all mining activity had stopped. The price of Cobalt had slipped to under $10 a pound. Noranda seeked political support from Idaho Legislators for passage of HR 5540, Defense Industrial Base Revitalization Act. This act would provide government price supports for critical minerals, including cobalt. Noranda continued to operate the water treatment plant and town site maintenance was curtailed. Jack "Buzz" Miller, the informal mayor of Cobalt retired.

Environmental Restoration Begins

Environmental Restoration and Recovery 1970 to 1983

Restoration of the Panther Creek Drainage, including Blackbird Creek started in the 1970, when the Forest Service removed mine tailings from 5,800 feet of the lower reach of the creek. Prior to the 1930s, mill tailings were often dumped directly into the creek according to a 1985 study. This restoration also included an effort to grow a grass cover on the open pit spoils piles.

Upper spoils dump, with grass growing on the surface. (Photo provided by Teddy Miller)

LEGAL ACTION TAKEN AGAINST MINE OWNERS 1983 TO PRESENT

In 1983, the State of Idaho initiated a natural resources damage assessment, or NRDA for short, requiring the Blackbird Mine to clean up pursuant to CERCLA. From 1983 through 1986, the only activity at the Blackbird was the treatment of the acid water, laden with heavy metals, flowing from the mine. The water was treated with lime and released into Blackbird Creek.

In April, 1987, the Ninth U.S. Circuit Court of Appeals ruled that the State of Idaho could sue past operators of the Blackbird Mine for environmental damages to the Panther Creek drainage. The State alleged that Noranda Mines, Ltd., Noranda Exploration Inc., Hanna Mining Co., and Hownet Turbine Corp. were responsible for mine-related water pollution, seeking $25 million in damages.

BLACKBIRD METALS COMPANY 1988-1990

Mid year 1988, Blackbird Metals Co., a New York-based partnership, announced plans to buy the mine. They planned to invest $85 million in the project, with $47 million for an offsite refinery, and 7 million to the State to settle the lawsuit against previous owners. The price of Cobalt is about $7.00 a pound.

In 1989, Blackbird Metals Co. was still optomistic the mine could be opended and they would find the money for the offsite refinery and the State would settle the environmental judgement for $7 milloion dollars. They soon lost interest as the environmental problems continued to mount and more law suits were on the horizon.

In 1992, the State of Idaho filed an action under CERCLA and passed various Idaho Laws to clean up the site, including the adjoining creeks and restore the natural environment. Soon after the initial filing, the U.S. government joined the suit bringing it under CERCLA, the Clean Water Act, and the Endangered Species Act. In 1995, Consent Decree was lodged against the defendants, the Blackbird Mine Site Group (Noranda Mining Inc., M.A. Hanna Co. and Alumet Corporation.)

In 1993, an Emergency Response Action was issued to clean up the West Fork of Blackbird Creek Tailing Impound. These actions were necessary as storm waters were exceeding the capacity of the culvert under the tailings, resulting in tailings being forced over the spill way into Blackbird Creek and Panther Creek. There was also growing concern if the culvert were to become clogged, the whole structure could be compromised, flooding both streams with millions of gallons of contaminated tailings. The emergency response was to build a lined channel for the creek to flow over the tailings and build a new spillway.

From 1995 to 2003, additional actions were issued to clean up the acid rock drainage that was impacting water quality. Water leaching through the spoils piles was carrying heavy metals into Bucktail Creek, Meadow Creek and the Blackbird Creek drainages.

In 1994, the Mill was salvaged and equipment sent to Cannea, Mexico. A Federal judge ruled that Noranda and Alumet would have to pay for the Blackbird cleanup.

In 1995, Noranda, Machinery Center, Inc.;. M.A. Hanna Company, Alumet Corp (the Blackbird Mine site group) and Union Carbide agreed to clean up the site. Estimated cost was $24-$53 million to stabilize 4.8 million tons of rock, 2 million tons of tailings, and an 11.5 acre open pit. Cobalt price was $28 per pound.

MORE BLACKBIRD DISTRICT WEALTH

IDAHO COBALT PROJECT

According to the 2000 U.S. Geological Survey Minerals Yearbook, The Formation Capital Corp. had the most significant metal exploration project in Idaho in 2000. The company continued work on its Idaho Cobalt Project, formerly the Sunshine Project, just north of the Blackbird. The company believes the Idaho Cobalt Belt still contains large quantities of high grade cobalt. This belt of cobalt is one of only two high-grade reserves of this strategic metal in the United States. Formation Capital Corp has 137 unpatented claims on which it has been exploring since 1993. Most of the work in 2000 involved offsite feasibility studies and permitting activities, though the company did drill eight metallurgical test holes on its Ram deposit.

Feasibility studies by Mine Development Associates, based on the more than 100 diamond drill holes, have indicated favorable economics for a small underground mine. The proven and probable reserve is listed

Concrete mill foundations (Photo by the author, 2006)

at 1.55 million tons of 0.695% cobalt, 0.54% copper, and a gold credit, with substantial exploration potential at depth, along strike zones, and district wide.

Formation Capitol Corporation has submitted a plan for the Idaho Cobalt Project to the US Department of Agriculture. This plan includes the

Big Flat to the North of the historic Blackbird Open Pit (Source, Google Earth)

development of two underground mining operations from two different deposits. The Ram deposit and the Sunshine deposit. Output from both will be processed by a single flotation mill located on the Big Flat area between Big Deer Creek and Little Deer Creek. Facilities on the Big Flat will include water treatment plant, offices, warehouses, change rooms, shipping and receiving docks, emergency sleeping quarters and other structures. The project will be done in three phases. The construction phase is expected to last two years. The operating phase ten to twelve years, with a gradual ramp up from 440 tons per day to 800 tons per day as the Ram mine expands. The reclamation/closure phase is expected to last two years, followed by thirty plus years of post mine treatment and monitoring.

Rather than build a town site, employees and supplies will be bussed and trucked in via Williams Creek, Deep Creek and then up Panther Creek to Blackbird Creek. Access to the FCC site will be through the decommissioned Blackbird Mine site.

Anticipated employment during the initial phase of production is 69, increasing to 105 at full production. The mill is expected to employ about 31 people, bringing the total project employment to approximately 157.

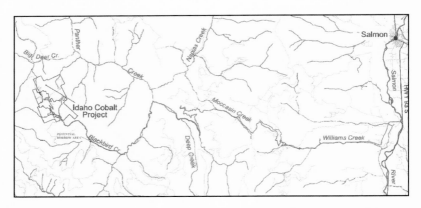

Map of FCC's Idaho Cobalt Project Site [Source, USDA Draft Environmental Impact Statement]

Rather than utilize tracked ore trains used in the Blackbird, the Idaho Cobalt Project will use diesel powered 20-ton trucks which will access both the Sunshine and Ram portals using inclined ramps. A tram will be built to bring ore from the Ram portal to the mill site on the Big Flat. Sunshine ore will be trucked directly to the mill from the portal. Extensive measures are planned to insure that water quality is not compromised, including monitoring wells, water management ponds, drainage collection system, including the covering of spoils piles to limit infiltration of rain and snow runoff into the spoils piles.

This is an ambitious project to recover more of the Blackbird Mining District's mineral wealth. Modern versions of the miners that came to the region in the 1890s seeking gold and copper, with far more environmental restrictions than those early miners. While technology has reduced the cost of mining, the environmental regulations have increased the risk for future economic success.

COBALT

A COMPANY MINING TOWN

AUCTION
COBALT MINING TOWNSITE
COBALT, IDAHO

PLEASE POST!   *PLEASE POST!*

Buildings, Houses, Contents & Misc.
PREVIEW FRIDAY, AUGUST 21ST
SATURDAY, AUGUST 22, 1987 - 10:00 A.M.
SUNDAY, AUGUST 23, 1987 - 10:00 A.M.
LOCATION: ON SITE COBALT, IDAHO

DIRECTIONS FROM SALMON: 5 Miles South on Highway 93. Turn right, cross river bridge. Follow road over Williams Creek Summit to Panther Creek. Turn left, follow road to Cobalt. Routes will be marked.

DIRECTIONS FROM CHALLIS: 8 Miles North of Challis, turn left on Morgan Creek Road. Follow main Morgan Creek Road to Cobalt. Route will be marked.

HOUSES AND BUILDINGS:

SEWER SYSTEM & ELECTRIC PLANT & FIRE EQUIPMENT:

TOOLS & EQUIPMENT:

COMMERCIAL KITCHEN, LAUNDRY & CLEANING EQUIPMENT:

RECREATION EQUIPMENT:

HOUSEHOLD & FURNITURE:

SODA FOUNTAIN EQUIPMENT:

ELECTRIC, PLUMBING, AND BUILDING SUPPLIES:

OFFICE FURNITURE:

MISCELLANEOUS:

SALE CONDUCTED BY . . .

ACK'S AUCTION SERVICE
DALE ACKERMAN, Auctioneer

ALL ITEMS TO BE SETTLED FOR DAY OF SALE — CASH OR APPROVED CHECKS WITH I.D.

PHONE 208-756-4980
ROUTE 1 BOX 222   SALMON, IDAHO 83467

Auction Announcement (Picture from author's collection of original poster at the Lemhi County Historical Society)

54

Chapter One—Remembering Cobalt

"Hey, Russ we're too late, they're tearing the place down," announced Darrin, my daughter's boyfriend and future husband, over the CB radio. "Guys are throwing stuff off the building roof at 2 o'clock.

In 1988, I brought my wife Ellen, three of our four daughters, one daughter's boy friend, and Anne Hanna, my wife's sister to, Cobalt, to show them the stage where all my "growing up in Cobalt" stories took place. But, we found the town in shambles, empty foundations, partly dismantled buildings, and piles of trash. Cobalt had been sold at auction and the buyers were taking away their booty. We did not know Cobalt had been sold at auction, before planning our trip.

Our two-car caravan stopped at the abandoned service station at the center of town. The last gas pumped was ten gallons at $0.34 cents per gallon. It was lunch time and the workers stopped ripping boards from the bunkhouse walls and roof of the recreation hall, and took a break.

Cobalt service station 1988. (Photo by Ellen Steele)

We slipped into the Recreation Hall, and returned to the 1950s. The bowling shoes were still in cubbies behind the counter, my favorite red and black bowling ball was on the return ball rack, the aroma of oil treated alleys came from behind the folding security screen. A rack of balls were on the pool table, broken cue sticks leaning against the wall.

The pinball machines were long gone, memories filling in the blank spaces where they once stood against the wall, lights flashing, bells ringing as the steel balls ricoched from post to post, the flippers clacking like castanets, the player banging the machine against the wall, when the ball failed to drop in the money hole.

A 1988, photo of the Recreation Hall and the back of two heads, the author's youngest daughter, and the balding author. (Photo by Ellen Steele)

Sneaking up the stairs, the bar still smelled of cigarettes and spilled beer. The cafe was locked, but counter and stools looked ready for customers, the jukebox waiting for a dime. Across the hall in the theater and gym, the basket ball hoops waiting for a pick up game. High above the floor, on the back wall, the projection booth stood empty, the powerful arc projectors long gone, sold at auction. Closing my eyes, I could hear the cowboys chasing the indians at the Saturday afternoon movie. We had cowboy movies every Saturday, and sometimes I ran the projector for the part time projectionist, one of the miners.

Panther Creek Inn with weeds at the door, 1988 (Photo by Ellen Steele)

My memories were being trashed along with the town, and everyone was hungry, so we did not stay long. Our original plan was to have burgers and fries at the Panther Creek Inn, like in the old days. But, it was closed, a For Sale sign on the door.

We ate a backup lunch of candy bars, some potato chips, carrot and celery sticks at the Clear Creek Campground. We went to Salmon for ice cream before returning to our camp site at Redfish Lake. I took the whole party up Napias Creek, to see for themselves the steep narrow road, with shear rock walls on one side and a thousand foot drop to the rocks below on the other. I asked them to imagine the road covered with ice and snow.

Later that night, leaning into the coals of a dying campfire, I savored my last cup of coffee and wondered, what happened to all our Cobalt neighbors? The people who built Cobalt in the 1950s? Who were the miners and their families that tried to sustain Cobalt in the 1960s, and those who rebuilt the town in the early 1980s, hoping to reopen the mine? Who bought our first house, the company buildings, the Recreation Hall? When did the IGA Market close? Did other families have fond memories of Cobalt? Did they have stories to share? I hope I can answer these questions in future chapters and on the Internet. I have many collected stories and photos of the people who built the town and worked at the Blackbird Mine. Too many for a single volume, so I will publish them on the web at Cobalt Memories.

In the 1940s, miners came seeking jobs at the Blackbird, as did my family in 1949, and again in 1956, after returning to California for five years. Together, the miners built homes, schools, created church groups, and built a community in the wilderness. The miners and families formed strong bonds wrought by common hardships and the challenges of living in a National Forest meadow along Panther Creek, far from a real town with electricity, phones and radio stations.

For many families their Cobalt roots became deeply entangled in the rich meadow soil, like the willow roots on the banks of Panther Creek. Some held semi annual reunions for sixteen years after the Blackbird mine closed in 1959. Other restless miners moved on without looking back, just like those who came in the early 1900s. Over the next thirty years, multiple attempts were made to re-open the mine and revive Cobalt.

Some "Cobalters" fought to keep their ninety-nine year leases after the town was sold; even though there was no electricity, running water, or sewer. The Hill family returns to their Cobalt home each summer so their children can experience Cobalt's unique magic. Over the years, I also returned several times with my own family, in 1988, 1994 and 2001, to refresh my childhood memories and to have one more hamburger at the Panther Creek Inn. Cobalt was a magical place to grow up.

Psychologists tell us that moments of high emotion are those most likely to remain locked in our memories. I am harvesting these memories as truthfully as I can and have asked other Cobalt residents to share their memories and photographs. Together, we can save the memories of Idaho's last company town for future generations to share.

South end of town site in 1952. (Photo provided by Lyle Greig)

CHAPTER TWO
THE STEELE FAMILY AT THE BLACKBIRD

Family picture, Bert and Margaret Steele, with their boys Russell left, Robert right, and Ronald standing, just before coming to Idaho.

My Idaho history started in 1949 on a warm July evening in the Sierra Nevada foothills. Sunset shadows were creeping across my Grandmother Frances Thomas' yard, a summer breeze pushed the day's heat back into the Central Valley of California. "The three Steele boys were sitting on the back steps of Grandmother Thomas' shingled cottage, built from material salvaged from Beale Army Air Corp base.

We had just moved in with Grandmother, as Mom and Dad had plans to build a house on seven acres next door. A house big enough for three growing boys, enough land for cows, horses, pigs, sheep and some chickens.

Ron, the youngest, a round-faced seven year-old, had a mischievous grin, snow-white blond hair and hazel eyes. "Very independent, did not like to be told more than once to do something," according to our Mom. Bob in the middle, a sharp featured nine year-old, with a large nose, dark almost black hair and hazel eyes. "He was a big tease and a hard worker, but hated school," said Mom. The oldest at eleven, my most distinguishing features were freckles and big ears that stuck out like wings. According to my mother, "You were a good student, fascinated by anything electrical. We had to ban you from touching flashlights, toasters, radios and clocks. "

We were snapping beans from Grandmother's garden. Each of us had a bowl between our knees. A paper bag of freshly picked string beans on the step. We were snapping off the tips, pulling the strings, then snapping them into one inch pieces, for canning.

Bob threw a hand full of tips and strings at me. The scuffle brought Grandma Frances to the kitchen door, wiping her hands on the ever-present gingham apron, before pushing back the graying ginger curls on her forehead. "No throwing! Beans in the bowl, tips in the bag, not in your brothers face," she said. She wasn't much

Francis Thomas had a big influence on the Steele Boys.

taller than I was at eleven, about five feet, but I didn't feel like getting hauled in the kitchen by my ear for a tongue-lashing. I was rather looking forward to the strawberry rhubarb pie she had just popped in the oven. We had picked the strawberries and rhubarb from a patch near the garage, earlier that morning.

"Listen!" I said, breaking the tension. In the silence, we could hear a heavy vehicle coming up the hill behind the house, brakes protesting as it stopped in the driveway. "Dads home, Dads home," we shouted to Grandmother. "It's not Bert, he's forty miles from here in Forest Hill," replied Grandmother.

Dropping our bowls, we all ran to see if it was Dad's truck, a war surplus army vehicle with an open cab, converted to haul logs. We bumped into him, as he came around the corner of the garage. "Lets go get your Mom in Idaho," he said with a big grin. " The Forest Service shut down login' until it rains."

Our mother Margaret, the oldest of the four Thomas children, was helping

Bert Steele and Army Surplus Logging Truck (Photo by Margaret Steele)

her youngest sister Hazel Whitford move to Idaho with two small children, Bill was twenty four months and Mary nine months. Uncle Fred Whitford had just graduated from the University of Nevada's Mackay School of Mines in Reno, and had taken his first job at the Blackbird Mine, in the Salmon National Forest.

Coming into the house, Dad asked, "Francis, can you get these boys some clean clothes?" In the kitchen, Grandmother wiped her hands on her cotton apron. "We haft'a leave tonight," he explained. "We haft'a get to Salmon before Maggie catches the bus on Saturday." My mother's given name was Margaret, but to Dad she was Maggie.

In his youth, Dad was a handsome five foot ten, with a James Dean-like smolder and slicked back dark brown hair and hazel eyes. He rode motorcycles and wore leather jackets, smoked Camels, and exuded an air of danger. Dad had been a B-25 Pilot in WWII and had wanted to stay in the military, but Mom wanted to raise her boys in California, not in occupied Germany. He resigned from the Air Force and bought a war surplus Army 6 x 6 and used his shipyard welding skills to build a logging truck. He became a contract log hauler.

With no logs to haul, Dad was intent on rescuing our Mom from a long bus ride home. A scheme he had hatched over several beers at Ed Frano's pub, before coming home smelling of beer and cigarettes. It was getting dark when we climbed in the family sedan, a green 1947 Studebaker with sticky seats. With me riding shotgun in the right front, Ron and Bob in the back seat, we headed up Highway 20 to US 40, now I-80, in the dark. We were three guys on a road trip with their Dad.

We did not know it then, but we were on an adventure that would shape our lives forever, and produce hundreds of often told stories which began, "When I was growing up in Idaho, or when we lived in Cobalt."

I do not remember much of our trip across the Nevada desert, other than it was hot, the sun bouncing off white sand, dusty brown rocks, gray sage brush gullies, and purple mountains shimmering in the distance. Every couple of hours a fight would break out over who was sitting where, as if a seat change would reduce the sweat generating heat. I was determined to hang on to my front seat position, which had a window wing and an air scoop that funneled air under the dash. Dad showed us how to wet our T-shirts from the water bag hung on the bumper, and let the air coming in the open windows and vents cool us.

A 1947 Studebaker Commander similar to Steele Family Car

Dad stopped only for gas, food, and coffee. I remember one station had a red Coke machine and we begged for dimes. I rubbed the cold bottle on my face and neck, before popping off the top, savored that first swallow, letting the foam dissolve the wind blown crud on my tongue.

By early evening, we had crossed into Idaho from Nevada near Jackpot, and the center line changed from white to orange. As the sun sank behind the mountains, we could see black clouds on the horizon. An occasional lightning flash backlit the vertical wall of clouds sweeping down from the mountains.

Darkness enveloped us with only the headlights and flashes of lightning to guide Dad down Highway 93 into the Arco Desert. Coming closer, lightning bolts leaped from the ground into the rolling cauldron of wind and rain in front of the Studebaker. "Gezess Christ, look at that," exclaimed Dad, as a glowing ball of energy bounced across the road.

"Christ, now it's raining mud," muttered Dad as he turned on the wipers. Though not a religious man, my father always called for Christ's help when things went wrong. The wipers smoothed the mud across the glass as expertly as Mother buttered a cake with chocolate frosting. He could no longer see the road. Creeping to side of the road Dad reached under the seat, grabbed a rag he kept there for wiping the dipstick, then rolled down the driver's window to wipe the windshield, but the mud kept falling, covering his arm and the side of his face.

He rolled up the window, wiping off the mud with the dirty rag. As we sat on the side of the road, rain and hail hammering the car, a chill broke the summer heat. Lightning leaped from the black top only yards in front of the Studebaker, then again from the lava flow to our right. I refused to look any more, putting my head on my knees. I could smell hot iron and charcoal in the air coming through the vent under the dash.

The mud soon turned to dirty water and Dad started the engine, driving down a rain-drenched tunnel of light, and turned into the Craters of the Moon National Monument, seeking shelter. All the lights were out and no one answered Dad's pounding on the door. Returning to the car, Dad suggested we get some sleep. I woke up cold and hungry as the sun was creeping over the mountains to the east, casting long shadows on the jumbled lava crust that filled the valley floor.

We stopped for a breakfast of donuts, coffee and hot chocolate in Arco. With a recharged thermos of coffee on the seat next to Dad, we were back on the road. Wisps of fog hovered over the puddles, as the sun heated the blacktop. Dad topped off the Studabaker's gas tank in Challis and asked the attendant how far to the William Creek turn off? "About five miles before you get to Salmon," he said.

We missed the turn off the first time, turning around on the edge of Salmon across from the indian log houses, retracing our tracks. On our second try, we found the William's Creek Forest Service road, crossed the Salmon river on a rickety bridge, traveling parallel to the river on rolling hills covered in gray sage brush; then we made a sharp right into the willow choked William's Creek Canyon. Along the creek we caught glimpses of cabins hiding in the willows. Going west, we climbed up the mountain, switch back by switch back, over washboard roads that caused our teeth to clack when we tried to talk. Looking over the edge, I could see our dust settling on the road directly below, no guard rails to keep a car from plunging down the mountain.

Rounding the big bend at Cougar Point Campground, Dad pulled over to let a car pass in the other direction. We recognized "Willie," Uncle Fred's green Chevrolet. As the two cars passed, we could see our Mother waving wildly to us from the passenger seat. Aunt Hazel, Bill and Mary were in the back. Uncle Fred went past us, his wheels skidding in the dust. Mom was beaming, she had been saved from a two day bus ride home to California.

After all the hello's and catching up, we went in to Salmon. Dad surprised us at lunch by declaring he wanted to stay in Idaho if he could get a job. Questions came from all directions. Mom was concerned about leaving her family in Nevada City. Dad was quick to point out her sister would be just down the street. Bob and Ron thought moving to Idaho was a great idea, they had already heard two of Uncle Fred's fish stories. I was scared, we had just moved to Grandmother's house, now we were going to move again!

With the decision made, Dad and Uncle Fred discussed jobs in the Salmon Hotel bar over a beer. "They are building an underground maintenance shop and might need a mechanic," said Uncle Fred. With both cars brimming with supplies from the Harris's grocery store, we headed back to the Blackbird mine, retracing our route back up Steven's Creek, across the 8,000 foot summit and then down Moccasin Creek to Napias Creek, where the road narrows and is quite steep. The sight of many deadly accidents over the years.

Dad followed Uncle Fred's lead and honked his horn at each blind corner. In mid summer, it was 39 miles of dusty washboard road, carved out of steep slopes covered with Lodge Pole Pine and Douglas Fir, mixed with Aspen groves at the higher elevations. By the time we got to Panther Creek, it was dusk. We could only see one light on at the new town site. The Panther Creek Inn, a hangout for miners and sportsmen, had the lights on, but Uncle Fred did not stop, turning west into the Blackbird Creek Canyon, just beyond the lights.

Our destination was still six miles up Blackbird Creek. We followed Willie's headlights, sliding along the sharp talus-strewn mountainside as Uncle Fred navigated the twisty road to the mine, past the dark sawmill, the beaver ponds, ever upward. After a while we could see lights farther up the canyon. We had arrived at the Blackbird, like so many earlier miners who came to the Blackbird canyon in the late 1800s and early 1900s.

In Willie's headlights was a small log cabin, half buried in the hillside. It was caulked with oakum and concrete to keep out the winter wind, the

The log cabin, with Cousin Bill Whitford on the steps, with his mother looking on from the doorway. (Photo from Hazel Whitford's private collection.)

mice and rats, looking for a warm winter hideaway, or so we thought. The front porch of rough sawed planks sagged into the road which was only a few feet from the cabin door. To enter you pulled on a leather string to lift a wooden latch. A metal roof kept out the rain and snow.

Getting out of the Studebaker we were drafted by Aunt Hazel to carry in supplies, which we stacked on the rough drain board under the single window facing the morning sun. Dad and Uncle Fred disappeared into the dark with a flashlight, to return minutes later with two World War II army bunks, 30-inch wide cots on stilts. They had liberated them from a barracks building behind the cabin, one of the mine bunkhouses which shared this wide spot in the road at the entrance to the mine.

The next morning, Sunday, we drove to the town site for a windshield survey. On the north end of the meadow, Calera Mining Company was building white company houses, trimmed in Forest Service green. In the center of town the power plant, bunk and cookhouses were under construction. Employee housing was at the south end of the meadow, where several private homes were under construction.

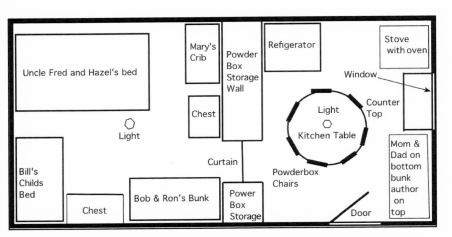

Blackbird Miners log cabin floor Plan, used by Whitford and Steele Families, July to November 1949. [Graphic by author]

By Monday noon, Dad had secured the underground mechanic's job and we were on our way back to California to collect our belongings. We were moving to Idaho to live in the log cabin with Uncle Fred and his family. Nine of us in a small cabin, smaller than the basement bedroom my brother and I had in Grandmother's cottage in California. I wondered if we could really do it?

CHAPTER THREE

LIVING AT THE BLACKBIRD

"Jeezes Christ!" bellowed Dad in the dark, "I felt a rats tail in my mouth." Mom jumped out of the bottom bunk she shared with Dad and turned on the single bulb over the table in the center of the room. In the corner of our miners log cabin half buried in the hillside, was a large gray rat, red eyes darting about, and a naked tail longer than it's body wiggling on the dirt floor. Dad pulled up his knees on the lower bunk shouting, "don't let it up here, don't let it up here." Mom lifted the leather latch and opened the plank door, providing an inviting escape route for the rat.

The rat scampered under the refrigerator. Picking up a long handled meat fork from the sink counter, Mom got down on her knees, clutching the front of her white cotton nightgown with one hand and jabbing under the refrigerator with the other, encouraging the rat to make a break for freedom.

Bill Whitford with his Dad's engineers pick, at the back of the cabin. In the distance one of the CCC building apartments. (Photo by Hazel Whitford)

A storage wall of empty wooden powder boxes stacked to the ceiling and a curtain divided the cabin. On the other side my cousins Bill and baby Mary, woke up and were crying. My brothers Bob and Ron, in their own bunk bed behind the wall, were calling for Mom.

Aunt Hazel was shrieking, "What's wrong, what's wrong?" Dad continued his "not up here" litany from the bunk below me. From my perch on the top bunk, I was silently agreeing with Dad, "not up here."

Uncle Fred, wearing only a t-shirt and boxer shorts, charged through the storage wall curtain, his engineer's rock pick held high.

Tired of dodging the fork, the rat made a run for the door right across Uncle Fred's path. Wham! He nailed the rat to the dirt floor with the sharp end of the pick. Stepping on the rat's tail, Uncle Fred pulled the pick from its brain and returned to bed without uttering a word. Mom scooped the twitching rat up with the dustpan and hurled it into the night, putting a dishtowel over the bloody spot on the floor. Mom re-latched the door and turned off the light, bumping into a powder box stool as she made her way back to bed. Soon Mom and Dad were breathing in synchronization again on the bunk below me. A little excitement for our first week at the Blackbird Mine.

We lived in the rat and mouse infested cabin for four months, while Dad and Mom built a more modern log cabin at the town site. As the weather got colder, more of the critters tried to move in where it was warm and food was plentiful.

One morning I reached through the curtain under the sink into a basket of apples without looking, and grabbed a mouse. Mom had bought a basket of apples from a truck garden vendor, and was storing them under the sink. In my surprise I jumped back and bumped my head on the kitchen table, while the mouse made its escape. Mom set two traps every night. If anyone was awake, they could hear one or more of the traps go off before dawn.

The miners cabin was built about 1900, but it had been given a 20th century upgrade. Two overhead lights, one in each room, and a propane range with an oven. We brought the refrigerator with us from California. The electricity came from a generator up by the 6850 portal. We carried water in buckets from a faucet across the road, dumped the waste water in the road and used the school house outhouse for sanitation breaks. Baths were taken in a laundry tub in the middle of the kitchen.

The school was in one end of a portable barracks building, which had been hauled up from an abandoned CCC camp on the Salmon River. The classroom was in one end and the teacher, Mrs. Morrison, lived in the other end with her wimpy husband and seven year old son. The whole one room school was heated by a balky oil stove that often broke into whooping fits, blowing soot balls into the room, as it threatened to explode. Mrs. Morrison would start screaming for one of the fifth graders to turn off the oil, while she shooed the first, second and third graders to safety through her quarters, waking her husband who worked nightshift. We did not have any fourth graders and the three fifth graders exited out the front door, after turning off the oil. After an hour on the play ground the oil smoke cleared and Mrs. Morrison tried to light the oil stove again with wads of news paper soaked in the oil, before we all froze to death on the play ground.

In the winter the play ground equipment was so cold you could not touch it with bare hands, or you would stick to the metal until the teacher came with a pot of hot water, to get you loose.

Inspecting the Steele house foundation at lot 26 in September 1949.

By September, Dad had secured a lease on lot 26 at the town site and a $2,500 loan from the mine to start a house. Each family was given a 99 year lease and an opportunity get a loan and authorization to purchase through the mine procurement office.

Every night Mom, Dad and Uncle Fred went to the town site to work on our house along with other men living in the bunk house behind the cabin, who were also building at the town site. One was Walt Lea, a mine electrician, who was building on lot 25 next to us.

The miners all helped each other. Uncle Fred built chimneys. Dad, a pipe fitter, did the plumbing, Walt, an electrician did the wiring. Mom often went to the town site while we were in school to work on the house. Mom nailed up sheet rock and nailed down the tounge and groove oak floors. Aunt Hazel baked pies, cakes or cookies while she watched Bill and Mary, and helped us with school home work in the cabin. After all the kids were in bed, the house builders crowded into the small cabin for coffee, and Aunt Hazel's fresh baked cookies and coffeecake.

I often wondered about the other families who lived at the mine. What were the very early days like, when the Calara was just getting started.

New log building in 1940s, thought to be the cook house and office. (Photo provided by Idaho Geological Survey)

Blackbird buildings, possibly the Bunkhouse and Essay Office, 1940. (Photo provided by Idaho Geological Survey)

Chapter Four

The Early Days at the Blackbird

Mining is hard dangerous work, often in remote areas far from the comforts of town and family. Early miners pitched their tents on the claim and slept on the ground each night, leaving their family in nearby towns. As a claim progressed from gopher hole to a shaft or tunnel in the hillside, more workers were needed. Bunk and cook houses were built. This was also true at the Blackbird.

In the late 40s, Blackbird miners lived in an unheated bunkhouse, dipping water from the creek for bathing and shaving. Jim Caples was originally hired as a miner, but was eventually promoted to timekeeper and purchasing agent when Ed Douglas, the Mine Manager, discovered he could type. A skill he learned in the Army. "I would muck all day and type reports at night," said Caples. "As we hired more miners, I became the time keeper and purchasing agent. Eventually I was doing most of the hiring."

The bunkhouse was one long room, with space for twelve bunk beds. "In the winter the snow filtered through the cracks in the walls," said Caples. Before the mine shower facility was built, the miners had to dip water from the creek and heat it on the top of an oil stove. In the winter, the first miner up each morning had to chop a hole in the ice to dip water. "We had two trout living in the pool, we named them Minnie and Mickey" said Caples. "We had to warn the new guys not to scoop up Minnie and Mickey when they got water for washing up and shaving."

Adversity is said to be the mother of invention. "In the winter, with no insulation in the walls, the oil heater was on all the time. I asked Ed Douglas if we could buy some copper tubing to put in the stove pipe," said Caples. "We coiled the copper in the stove pipe, piped in water from up the creek and in the morning we had hot water."

Bunk house privacy was limited, evening poker games often went well into the night. One night one of the miners wanted to get some sleep, but the players continued to make rowdy card game noises. Going outside to visit the out house, the sleepy miner cut one end off a stick of dynamite, stuck a fuse in it with no cap. Before coming back in he lit the short fuse and as he came through the door, dropped the sputtering fuse and dynamite on the table. Seeing the burning fuse, the card players panicked and ran into the night. The miner shut the door, blocked it and went to bed. The fuse had no explosive cap and burned out without setting off the dynamite. Banging on the door, the poker-playing miners all promised to end the game and turn out the lights if he would let them back in. They were freezing without coats and boots.

Caples remembers the food from the cookhouse was excellent. "Mary Bradley was the cook and she knew how to cook for large groups," said Caples. "Her donuts were a huge bonus."

But good food was not enough. The married miners soon tired of bunk house living. They wanted to go home to the family each night, not a noisy bunk house which lacked privacy. They sought places where they could find rudimentary shelter for their families, old log cabins built by earlier miners, hunter and fishing cabins on lower Blackbird Creek and up Panther Creek toward Forney.

Miner's Quonset Huts huddling in the Blackbird Creek Canyon (Photo provided by Forest Service)

The mine managers searched for housing alternatives, first importing some Quonset huts from Fort Lewis in Washington, eventually hauling portable barracks up from an abandoned CCC Camp on Squaw Creek, down on the Salmon River. The portable plywood buildings and some fixed buildings were left behind in remote areas when the CCC program was abandoned in 1942. At least six of these buildings were hauled to the Blackbird and converted into duplexes, one family at each end. Two were used as temporary bunk houses, another was Mrs. Morrison's one room school, with quarters in the rear.

In 1950, nine families lived at the mine, the wooden buildings and one house trailer. The Swanson's were one of those families, We found Gladys Swanson at the Lemhi County Historical Society in Salmon, where she was a docent.

As the screen door of the Museum slammed shut behind us a tall slender gray haired lady, sitting behind a large desk, rose to greet us. "Do you have information on Cobalt." I asked.

"I used to live there in the 50s," she replied, "Until my husband was killed in a snow slide in 1956."

Gladys Swansons' strong voice did not betray her 86 years, but her long slender fingers attested to years of hard work. As our conversation continued, it was clear the past fifty years had not dulled her memory of Cobalt.

The Swanson's were married in 1947, and the family moved to the Blackbird mine. "Swede" was a heavy equipment operator, clearing roads in the winter with a road grader and fighting fires with a cat in the summer.

Abandoned CCC Camp, thought to be Squaw Creek, Salmon River Canyon. (Photo provided by the Forest Service)

The six wood frame uninsulated employee houses at the mine had running water and oil heaters. "Our oil bill was deducted from our paycheck each month. I remember being upset when the price of oil went to 19 cents a gallon," recalls Gladys. "Pay was only about $12.00 a day."

"It was a good place to live, we were close to our neighbors. We played cards a lot," said Gladys. " Before the rec hall opened we would have Saturday night dances a the school house, everybody got pleasantly boozed up and had a good time." The school house at Cobalt opened in 1952, and the Rec Hall in 1955.

Due to the distance to Salmon, over 40 miles of snow-covered gravel road in the winter, the miners worked two weeks straight with four days off. "We shopped in Salmon, everyone had a big deep freeze. Most of us knew how to shop to keep our freezers full, but some people were always borrowing, a cup of sugar, flour, even steaks. We had one neighbor, who never gave back anything. But, I am not go to tell you which one."

A Quonset Hut with storage building attached, 1949 (Photo provided by Lyle Greig)

"I remember when Ted Olson was killed in a under ground accident. The miners usually rode a bus, but that day they came down the road single file past our place, not saying a word, recalls Gladys. "My clothes line was on pulleys, one end connected to the house, the other end to a tree across the canyon. It bothered me all my laundry was flopping over the road," said Gladys.

Not all the houses at the mine were as comfortable as the wood frame buildings. Some of the early arrivals at the mine lived in converted Quonset Huts. "We built walls and ceilings and covered them with wall board." said Jim Caples. "It was OK until spring came. During the winter the steam from cooking and body moisture worked its way through the ceiling panels and collected on the cold metal. In the spring the ice melted and rained back on those living in the huts."

In 1950, Cobalt's four room school house opened six miles down the mountain. " Ted and Lena Greig had a pickup with a cover over the back, benches down both sides. To keep our kids warm they put a wood stove in the back, between the benches," recalls Gladys. "I always worried about the children's safety, it would never be allowed today." It was not long before management found a bus to take the mine kids to school. Lena Greig drove the bus each day according to a Salmon Recorder-Herald story.

When we first moved to the town site in November of 1949, my mother would drive us and the two Carothers boys back up the hill to the school at the mine. That is until Ed Douglas, the Manager found out about it, then he arranged for Ward Carothers, one of the engineers, to come to work late and drive his two boys, my two brothers and I to school. Dad went to work extra early each morning then drove us home after school was out.

Front of Cobalt School with Parent Teachers Associations Members, 1950-1951.
(Photo is from Margaret Steele's collection)

In the Spring of 1951, Dad received a letter from the Air Force Reserve soliciting his interest in returning to active duty. To fly B-25s again was the dream of a life time.

One of the B-25 flown by my Dad at Douglas Field, Arizona in WWII.

At the time, he was doing contract logging for the mine sawmill. He quit, put our house up for sale, and loaded all our stuff on his logging truck and we headed back to California. We left behind many friends and my grandparents on Dad's side of the family. George and Anna Steele had come from Texas in the summer of 1950, and lived at the mine where George helped build the mill and then worked as the graveyard watchman.

It was a horrible trip back to California, We got caught in a spring blizzard in the Craters of the Moon, with a Jeep Station Wagon, and logging truck loaded with all our household things.

George and Anna Steele in 1954, shortly after moving back to Nevada County, CA from Idaho.

We were the last party to make it through that day. An hour trip took seven hours in the freezing cold and zero visibility. The sky was clear above, but the blowing snow obscured everything.

Several time's the wind pushed the light Jeep off the road and Dad had to pull it off a snow bank, and once out of a gully. We were fortunate the logging truck had chains and we could rescue the Jeep.

Mom had the flu when we left, and by the time we reached Reno, Nevada we all had it, and had to stop 90 miles from Grandma's house in Nevada County, California. But, our troubles were not over, we had one more blizzard going over Donner Pass.

CHAPTER FOUR: THE EARLY DAYS AT THE BLACKBIRD

By the time we reached California the Air Force Reserve had changed their minds, the Korean war was winding down. Plus, Dad was too close to the cut off age, and he had a family. The Air Force was looking for younger pilots with fewer attachments. Our grandparents in Cobalt missed us kids, and in the summer of 1953, Bob, Ron and I returned to Cobalt to visit our grandparents, who lived in one of the old CCC buildings at the Blackbird.

George and Anna Steele, date and location unknown

Chapter Five

The Summer of 1953 at the Blackbird

Right after school was out the summer of 1953, Grandpa and Grandma Steele called and invited us to return to Cobalt for the summer. I was not happy about returning to Idaho, as I was afraid my past as a wagon thief would catch up with me. More on this secret in future chapters. But, unable to reveal my secret, I rode sullenly in the back of our Jeep station wagon, hoping the engine would blow up and we could go back to Nevada City. It was almost dark when we arrived in Wells, Nevada at the truck stop motel. Mom looked for our grandparents car, but they were not there, so she checked in. My brothers kept looking out the motel window, excited about every car that drove by, until Mom made us all go to bed.

When we woke up, Grandpa's two door forest green Chevy was parked outside the motel room, with Grandpa and Grandma sleeping in the car. They had driven all night from the Blackbird to Wells, arriving just before dawn. "Your Grandma don't like the heat" explained Grandpa. "Let's eat breakfast, we need to get started before it gets too hot." At breakfast, I asked where was the "Pimp Mobile," and got rapped on the head by my mother for using rude language. "Sold it," was all Grandpa would say about the Lincoln Continental Cabriolet he won in a Texas Hold 'em poker game.

We kissed Mom goodbye, and hugged Aunt Dee, who was helping Mom with the driving from California, we climbed into the back of the Chevy for another summer at the Blackbird Mine.

We all napped while Grandpa drove across the Arco desert, some cool air was generated by a swamp cooler in the passenger window. Grandma sat next to Grandpa, like lovers on a date, out of the moist wind coming in the window. The mobile swamp cooler was a tube clamped to a partly rolled up window, with a coco fiber screen resting in a pan of water. Grandpa stopped and filled the pan every few hours, and gave us a drink from the water bags he had hanging on the front bumper.

With a rooster tail of dust behind us, we rolled up to the Panther Creek Inn at dusk. We could smell the hamburgers on the grill, even before Grandpa opened the heavy wooden door to the log building.

"Where you bin? We missed you and Dickey at the 4th of July party," said Bruno from behind the bar.

"Picking up the grandkids. We promised to take' em fishing and get' em some of Edna's burgers," replied Grandpa, reaching for the beers Bruno slid down the bar. Bruno knew his regular customers.

"Take a booth, boys," said Bruno, "Edna will take your order."

The aroma of cooking hamburger and deep fried potatoes seeped out of the kitchen, masking the faint bouquet of sour beer and once-used cigarette smoke. Smiling, Edna slid the plates on to the booth table. "Eat up," she said with a funny accent. On our plate were grill-roasted buns with hand made hamburger patties that spilled over the sides, two crisp leaves of iceberg lettuce . . . a jackstraw pile of long golden French fries. The standard for all future burgers and fries had been set for a lifetime. We were pouring catsup on the fries when Edna brought our Cokes in the old fashion glass bottles.

The Steele Boys, Russ, Bob and Ron taken in 1950.

During the day at the Blackbird, we played in the cut bank next to the bunk house, carving roads on imaginary highways into the hillsides with blocks of wood, pretending they were dozers and ore trucks. At night we played games at the kitchen table. There was no TV or radio, we left them behind in California.

"I'll see your two beans and raise ya five," said Grandpa, as he adjusted his green eye-shade and tossed seven wooden safety matches into the pile in the middle of the oilcloth covered kitchen table. "Too much for me" said Ron, with an impish grin. Bob scowled down his generous nose, looked at his hole card and folded without a word.

Without checking my hole card, trying my best to be a pro, I slowly counted out ten matches, "see ya and raise you three." "Call, three deuces beats two pair," said Grandpa, putting down his hand and raking in the matches.

Grandpa Steele, a small man, about five foot two, with a year round chestnut tan and black friar's fringe over his ears, and twinkling black eyes, was teaching us to play poker and the value of a poker face. No radio or TV, we played cards most nights, gin rummy or poker, using pinto beans for poker chips. Half way through our lessons Grandma cooked the beans with a ham hock for dinner, forced us to use safety matches for chips, which we continued to call "beans".

We each started with a hundred beans, the winner was the one with the most beans when it was time for bed. Grandpa was an accomplished poker player, giving us little slack after our initial lessons. He was a great bluffer, with a

Panther Creek Inn in 1956, hanging over Panther Creek
(Photo provided by Lyle Greig)

dead pan face. You could not tell if he had a royal flush or nothing. Play the card you are dealt, was Grandpa's philosophy, sometimes your only choice is to bluff. House rules, you had to call to see if someone was bluffing,

The one bedroom apartment was half of a barracks hauled up Panther and Blackbird Creeks to a flat spot near the mouth of Hawkeye Gulch on the east edge of the mining claim. One of several portable wooden buildings hauled to the mine from the Squaw Creek CCC Camp on the Salmon river. It had running water in the kitchen, and an oil stove heater. We slept on Army surplus cots, put up along the kitchen wall, taken down each morning.

Grandma was prone to bouts of depression, but was always happy when we visited. Spoiling us kids was her great joy, much to our Mother's chagrin. Her simple cotton dress or apron had a pocket for her Lucky Strikes and bar room matches. After finishing the dinner dishes, she would pull up a chair and watch us play, her cigarette smoke creating abstract shadows on the kitchen table as it floated toward the single bulb above the table. She always sat behind Ron, he was her favorite. I suspect she coached him on the sly.

As July faded into August, our five card stud, one down and four up, and seven card stud two down, and five up as playing improved hand by hand. I preferred seven card stud so I could hear Grandpa's rhythmic patter, calling out the cards, speculating on who had the winning hand, "Rusty has two pair, Ronnie's got two deuces, Bobby, nothing yet."

The game slowed when Grandpa told us about memorable hands when playing in card rooms from California to Texas.

My favorite was Grandpa winning the Lincoln in a West Texas card game.

The "Pimp Mobile," as a worldly friend called the handcrafted two door Lincoln Continental Cabriolet. Only 265 were built. It was apple green with a creamy white convertible top, matching leather seats, white wall tires, and extra large chrome bumpers. Lincoln Continental was inscribed in chrome on each side of the hood.

Grandpa was playing five card draw with oil field roughnecks and the owner of local oil wells, in a make shift card room behind a local bar in Texas. Grandma returned to their motel room when the bar closed, but the owner continued to bring more rounds of beer to the card players. On the final round, when it came time to draw, Grandpa raised and drew no cards.

Everyone folded, but the owner of the Pimp Mobile. He started his hand with two aces and and drew two queens. The beligerent Texan was sure he had the winning hand, and Grandpa was bluffing. With no money to cover the final raise, he put up the Lincoln. Grandpa asked him to put the title on the table. At first he refused, and Grandpa started to rake in the pot. "Damn you George, I want to see your hand," said the Texan. "Put the title on the table if you want to see me," said Grandpa. With the title on the table, Grandpa showed his full house, threes and duces. That night Grandma and Grandma put every thing they owned in the Lincoln's trunk and left for Idaho. They

This is a model of the Lincoln Continental Cabriolet

were sure the Texan would come looking for his Lincoln once he sobered up in the morning.

Grandpa worked the graveyard shift, watching the Blackbird mill. Coming home from the mill before we were up, Grandpa slept until noon. It was hard for us to play quietly. If we came too close to the house or made too much noise, Grandma would admonish us. "Shush now, George is sleeping. Go over there on the bank and play." The school yard equipment was gone, taken to the town site.

Grandpa George in the Texas oil fields.

Our main diversion was carving a network of roads with blocks of wood in the exposed dirt banks behind one of the barracks buildings, creating switch backs, stick bridges and rock circled parking lots for our make believe earth moving equipment.

On the best days after lunch, Grandpa's breakfast, we went on fishing, hunting and berry gathering trips up and down Panther Creek. On one trip, we picked choke cherries, little bright red cherries with huge seeds that left little room for the sour flesh under the ruby skin. Grandma boiled the cherries in a pan with a little water, releasing the juice. Spreading part of a cotton flour sack over a large bowl, Grandma tied a sting around the bowl, pushing on the cloth to form a white funnel, into which she poured the hot liquid filled with pits, floating stems and cherry pulp. Stirring it back and forth with a big wooden spoon, the red cherry juice ran into the bowl. She returned the juice to the pan, added sugar and heated it to a slow boil, stirring it constantly. When it cooled, we had cherry syrup for our breakfast cornmeal pancakes.

Corn meal pancakes were not my favorite breakfast, but it was better than Cheerios or shredded wheat with diluted canned milk. I did not like milk, and room temperature canned milk was worse yet. Always trying to please, Grandma would pour hot water over the shredded wheat briskets and I would spoon huge amounts of brown sugar on top of the warm wet wheat. No milk. Cheerios, I just ate dry, picking them out of the bowl with my fingers, washing them down with hot chocolate made from diluted canned milk and two scoops of chocolate mix to hide the stomach turning taste of canned milk.

Beyond corn bread baked in a cast iron frying pan, the next best use for corn meal was to dip fresh caught browns or rainbows in canned milk, roll them in the corn meal and drop then in a pan of hot bacon grease. Again, another lesson in survival cooking from Grandpa.

Returning from a day trip to Challis for supplies, Grandpa drove down a low bank, on to a grassy meadow, host to clumps of willows, and the upper reaches of Panther Creek. We could see it sparking in the late afternoon sun, between breaks in the willows. Opening the trunk, Grandpa took out his fishing pole, a small green tackle box, and cast iron frying pan. "You guy's collect some dry branches for a camp fire," instructed Grandpa. " I'm going to catch our dinner," as he plunged in the willow thicket along Panther

Creek. Pouting about not being included, we complained to Grandma, who was smoking Lucky Strikes in the front seat. We bet her that Grandpa could never catch enough fish for dinner with out our help. She reminded us to start collecting dead limbs for the fire, pointing to a small grove of firs at the edge of the meadow.

We piled the dry wood next to a rock ring filled with ashes from previous camp fires. With a wad of Shell roadmap from the glovebox for tinder, we stacked the limbs in a tepee, something we learned in Boy Scouts. As the sun was setting behind the trees on a far ridge, Grandpa emerged from the willows, with ten trout on a willow stick. Lighting one more Lucky Strike, Grandma leaned down and lit the fire before blowing out the match. "A man with a fishing pole will never go to bed hungry," remarked Grandpa, as he dipped the cleaned trout in canned milk and rolled them in corn meal on a paper plate, dropping them into the cast iron frying pan filled with hot bacon grease, resting on stones nestled in the coals. To this day, my favorite fish is fresh trout, rolled in corn meal, and pan fried in hot bacon grease.

Another day, after picking black berries along Panther Creek, just a few miles from the Salmon River, Grandpa spotted a rattler curled up in the dust along the road. Pulling to the side of the road, the took a .22 rifle from the trunk. In a single shot, he lopped off the snake's head. Grandpa, picked up the rattler by the tail, it was as long as he was tall, and dropped it in the trunk. We all picked up our feet and put them on the seat. A mile of so up the road, two praire hens were claimed by the .22 rifle and Grandpa's steady aim. "If a hungry man does not have many bullets, he makes every one count," said Grandpa, when questioned about his skill with the rifle. "We need to teach you boys how to shoot straight, someday." Grandpa ate the snake for dinner, while we had praire chicken. He claimed it tasted like chicken, I will never know, refusing to taste the snake, when he offered me a bite. I was glad Grandma fried the snake in a separate pan.

.... we learned how to play poker that summer in Cobalt, but the most important lesson, whether sitting at the poker table or coping with life's challenges, was that winners play the cards they are dealt to the best of their ability.

CHAPTER SIX

Chapter Six, and all subsequent chapters, can be found at Cobalt Memories on the Internet. You will need to register by sending an e-mail to cobaltmemories@ gmail.com with the registration code in the back of this book. I will add your e-mail to a list of approved readers, giving you online access to color photos and video clips.

All visitors to Cobalt Memories can read the text and the accompanying photos, however book buyers will have access to color photo and video clip libraries.

http://cobaltmemories.wordpress.com/

By using this online hybrid, we can present more stories in a contributing author's own voice, view color photos, and video clips, including historic movies converted to video.

Once you register at Cobalt Memories you can read all future chapters, and you can post comments on stories, or you can contribute your own Cobalt Memories. In the future, we hope to publish a CD with all the stories, including the additional pictures and video clips.

ABOUT THE AUTHOR

Russ Steele has been a freelance writer for trade, computer and science magazines since 1978. He has published articles in *Kilobyte, Science Probe, Amateur Radio Astronomy, Satellite Times, Monitoring Times, Capitol Journal, Trailer Life* and *Comstock's*. He has also written regular columns for *The Union Newspaper* and *Comstock's*, a regional business magazine. He is currently working on his second book project, which explores 50 years of technology innovation in Nevada County, California.

Russ lived in Cobalt, Idaho from 1949 to 1952, and again in 1956 and 1957. He graduated from Salmon High School in 1957, attended Idaho State College for two years before entering the Air Force, retiring as a Lt. Colonel. He has a Bachelor of Science degree in Social Science.

Russ, with his wife Ellen and four daughters, moved back to Nevada County, California in 1980, following his retirement from the Air Force. He was a project manager, strategic planner and advance product development manager for TRW from 1980 to 1996, and President/CEO of a non-profit internet service provider for 18 months following his retirement from TRW.

In addition to operating his consulting and writing business, Russ is a community service volunteer. He sits on the Boards of the Nevada County Economic Resource Council and Sierra Environmental Studies Foundation. He is also a Nevada County Transportation Commissioner.

ACKNOWLEDGMENTS

The following individuals and organizations contributed to this history of the Blackbird Mine, and I thank them for their assistance and enthusiasm in supporting this project.

Ellen Steele, Nevada City, California

Bob and Alberta Wiederrick, Salmon, Idaho

Jim Caples, Salmon, Idaho

Irene Allen, Taylorville, Utah

Ken Rodgers, Salmon, Idaho

Ted Maestretti, Salmon, Idaho

Teddy Miller, Salmon, Idaho

Ray Hawthorne Salmon, Idaho

Herb St. Clair, Salmon, Idaho (Deceased)

Lyle Greig, Kelso, Washington

Gladus Swanson, Salmon, Idaho

Margaret Steele, Nevada City, California (Deceased)

Clifford (Bang) Schofield, Salmon Idaho

Hazel Whitford, Nevada City, California

Dale Coffin, Noranda Corp, Toronto, Canada

Caitlin Steele-Williams, San Francisco, California

Idaho Geological Survey, Moscow, Idaho

Lemhi County Historical Society, Salmon, Idaho

Salmon National Forest, Salmon, Idaho

Salmon Chamber of Commerce, Salmon, Idaho

Salmon Public Library, Salmon, Idaho

Idaho State Historical Society, Boise, Idaho

The Insightworks
P.O. Box 1569
Nevada City California
530-273-8085
insightworks@mac.com
www.theinsightworks.com

You can order additional copies of this book using this form.

Checks or cash only.

_____Copies "Cobalt, The Legacy of the Blackbird Mine" at $14.95 each

Name:_____

Address:_____

City:_____ State:_____ Zip: _____

Telephone: (_____)_____

E-Mail Address:_____

Shipping and handling: $5.00 for first book, and $2.00 each additional book.

Thank you for your order!

Russell Steele

Welcome to Cobaltmemories!
No Access Code Required. Log on to this URL:
http://cobaltmemories.wordpress.com
and enjoy the rest of my book. *Russ*